Maine MEMORIES

MAINE LAKES & MOUNTAINS

Presented by the

Portland Press Herald

Est. 1862

Maine Sunday Telegram

What Maine reads.

Acknowledgments

We are pleased to present this volume of "Maine Memories: Maine Lakes & Mountains." This unique pictorial book is a publication of *The Portland Press-Herald/Maine Sunday Telegram*. However, it is the result of contributions made by many people and organizations from throughout our readership area.

We are indebted, first of all, to those early residents of this area who captured their times – our history – in photographs, and provided us with a glimpse into their lives. Secondly, all area residents are indebted to the many individuals who are committed to preserving our history in various libraries, museums, historical societies, archives and personal collections.

We are pleased to acknowledge the generous contribution of both time and photo archives from the following organizations:

Fryeburg Historical Society	Limington Historical Society	Sebago Historical Society
Fryeburg Public Library	Maine Historic Preservation Commission	Standish Historical Society
Gray Historical Society	Maine Historical Society	Warren Memorial Library
Harrison Historical Society	Maine State Museum	Windham Historical Society
Limerick Historical Society	Sanford Historical Committee	Windham Public Library

In addition, we would like to thank our readers for the generous contribution of images and information from their personal collections. There are many never-before-published images in this book. Many of these images and the corresponding information came from these personal collections. We would also like to thank Harland H. Eastman for his depth of knowledge on the Mousam Lake region and his willingness to allow us to draw on that knowledge and to quote liberally from the numerous books he has published on the area.

We also want to thank Maine State Historian Earle Shettleworth. In addition to contributing images from the wonderful archives of the Maine Historic Preservation Commission, Earle also assisted in reviewing rough drafts of all three Maine Memories volumes.

Grateful acknowledgment is made of the sources consulted in compiling the narrative for this book, which include the "Maine Almanac," by Jim Brunelle; "Maine: A Guide To The Vacation State," edited by Ray Bearse; "Maine's Historic Places," by Frank A. Beard and Bette A. Smith; "1982 State O' Maine Facts," edited by Carl Cramer; "Remember the Portland, Maine Trolleys," by Edwin B. Robertson; "Maine Trivia," compiled by John N. Cole; "Greater Portland Celebration 350," compiled and edited by Albert F. Barnes; "Portland," a publication of Greater Portland Landmarks Incorporated; and the Blethen Maine Newspapers news archives.

Published by Pediment Publishing, a division of The Pediment Group, Inc. www.pediment.com   Printed in Canada

Contents

$\mathcal{L}$en Libby Candies is thrilled to sponsor "Maine Memories: Maine Lakes & Mountains."

This book is a celebration of our region's past, and Len Libby Candies – which has been commemorating life's sweetest moments since 1926 – is proud to be part of that history.

We hope you enjoy this remarkable collection of vintage photographs, just as Len Libby has, for generations, delighted in crafting its handmade chocolates and candies.

Maureen T. Hemond

Maureen Hemond
Owner, Len Libby Candies

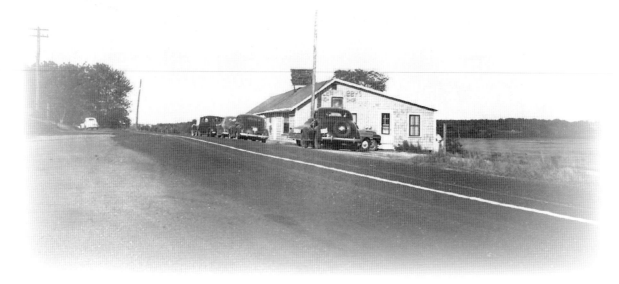

Foreword

These pages portray part of Maine as it was. And, in many rural and urban settings, as it still is. Throughout the creation of this unique book, there were moments when certain images had a singular ability to stop time and make the past present. We've discovered that although years have passed, the memories remain alive.

Maine is naturally a captivating state with an almost unlimited reserve of tales to tell. The *Portland Press Herald/Maine Sunday Telegram* had the opportunity to select but a few. In these stories, photographs and captions, we've journeyed into the 19th and early- and mid-20th century of the Maine lakes and mountains area to re-acquaint ourselves with its growth, daily realities, struggles and – most of all – its people. The result is a portrait that may strengthen our Maine ideals and offer a clearer image of who we are today.

We're grateful to the historical societies, museums and libraries that provided vital insight and direction, along with photographs from times past. Their cooperation and commitment ensured the completeness of this book.

We hope you enjoy your journey through "Maine Memories: Maine Lakes and Mountains." You may find it a familiar adventure.

Robert Bickler

Robert P. Bickler
President and General Manager
Portland Press Herald/Maine Sunday Telegram

One

Views & Street Scenes

We may never have walked these quiet village streets, or paused to admire the placid waterfront views depicted in the pages that follow. Yet these scenes from Maine's western lakes and mountain region are wonderfully familiar. All the flavor and charm of traditional, small-town New England life is here, from post-Civil War, horse-and-buggy days, to the decades before World War II and the coming of the automobile – a time when the local gas pump became as much a staple of village main streets as the town hall.

Here too are general stores, libraries, post offices and even blacksmith shops; farmhouses and taverns, Odd Fellows halls and carriage-makers. And, of course, rising amidst and above the trees' canopies, the handsome steeples of the village churches.

No less evocative are the figures who populate and enliven the photographs on these pages. Men idling on a storefront porch; families posing on what was undoubtedly an important occasion; groups of people gathered, with horses and wagons, as if having just arrived in town, or as if about to embark on a pleasure trip such as a lakeside picnic. We are indeed privileged to have a glimpse into their lives.

Left: View of Limerick, late 1880s. *Courtesy Sanford Historical Committee*

Right: Photograph of Main Street in Fryeburg taken by D. L. Lamson M.D. in 1865. *Courtesy Fryeburg Historical Society*

Above: Main Street, Standish, late 1800s. *Courtesy Standish Historical Society*

Above: A view of Main Street, Limerick, looking northwest in the late 1800s. *Courtesy Sanford Historical Committee*

Right: View of Bolsters Mills, Harrison, late 1800s. *Courtesy Harrison Historical Society*

Below: View of Standish, late 1800s. To the left is Route 25. To the right is Oak Hill. *Courtesy Standish Historical Society*

Above: East Waterboro town center, circa 1900. *Courtesy Sanford Historical Committee*

Left: View of Douglas Hill, Sebago, 1896. Geo. Douglas is unloading a wagon.
Courtesy Sebago Historical Society

Above: Standish Village view looking toward Oak Hill, late 1800s.
Courtesy Standish Historical Society

Right: West Newfield Village, early 1900s. Harold Moulton's store is on the left and the post office on the right. *Courtesy Sanford Historical Committee*

Right: View of Scribner's Mills, Harrison, 1906.
Courtesy Harrison Historical Society

Above: Congregational Church, Standish, early 1900.
Courtesy Standish Historical Society

Left: A view of Route 25 in Standish, circa 1910. *Courtesy F.H. Stickney*

Above: A view of Main Street Bridge in South Windham, circa 1905. *Courtesy Collections of the Warren Memorial Library*

Above left: View of the Commons, Harrison, early 1900s. Joe Pitts and later Carl Day's house is seen on the left. The tavern is straight ahead and the blacksmith shop is on the right. *Courtesy Harrison Historical Society*

Left: View of a main street in Cornish, 1900. *Courtesy Portland Press Herald*

Above: Two buildings on Portland Street in Fryeburg. The building on the right is shared by the United States Trust Company and E.E. Hastings, Attorney at Law.
Courtesy Fryeburg Historical Society

Right: View of Newfield, circa 1910.
Courtesy Sanford Historical Committee

Above: Main Street, Harrison, before the May 14, 1907 fire that would destroy these buildings. Pictured, left to right: J.F. Allen Shoe Store, Odd Fellows Building, Calvin Baptist Church, Jordan Stores, Coat Building and the Post Office.
Courtesy Harrison Historical Society

Right: The commercial block in Harrison Village before the 1907 fire. *Courtesy Harrison Historical Society*

Above: View of Sebago Center, (Mud City), Route 107, circa 1925. Back Nippin Road is on the right. *Courtesy Sebago Historical Society*

Left: View of Mud City, Sebago Center, circa 1925. This view is looking south to Mac's Corner.
Courtesy Sebago Historical Society

Above: View looking up Front Street, Harrison, early 1900s. The Bailey Block is on the left and a tavern is on the right.
Courtesy Harrison Historical Society

Right: View of the Harrison waterfront, early 1900s.
Courtesy Harrison Historical Society

Above: View of Coxes' Point, North Sebago, circa 1915. (It is the mouth of Bacheldor's Brook, where steamboats docked for passengers and freight). *Courtesy Sebago Historical Society*

Above: Public Library and Odd Fellows Block, Harrison, before the 1921 fire. *Courtesy Harrison Historical Society*

Right: Main Street at the corner of Depot Street, South Windham. The Oriental Hall is up on the right. *Courtesy Windham Historical Society*

Right: A view of the head of Long Lake in Harrison, circa 1915. *Courtesy Harrison Historical Society*

Below: Main Street, North Windham, circa 1920. Boody's store is on the left, as well as Tom Nason's store and Lizzie Pride's millinery shop. *Courtesy Windham Historical Society*

Above: View of Hog Fat Hill Road to Twin Lake House, Convene, circa 1924.
Courtesy Sebago Historical Society

Left: Nason's Brook, Steamboat Landing near Lake Croft Inn, North Sebago, circa 1925.
Courtesy Sebago Historical Society

Above: A view of Harrison, circa 1925.
Courtesy Harrison Historical Society

Right: Looking toward Sebago Lake from Hillcrest with the Sebago Lake Station in view and Indian Island in center, 1920s. *Courtesy Standish Historical Society*

Above: Aerial view of Fryeburg showing the Saco River in the distance, the First Congregational Church, Portland and Stuart streets. *Courtesy Fryeburg Historical Society*

Left: North Windham, looking toward Raymond, 1935. *Courtesy Windham Historical Society*

Above: New Portland Road looking north towards Gray corner. Because of the many hills on the Old Portland Road, it was decided to develop a New Portland Road where there were fewer hills. This was the primary road for traveling to and from Portland. Photo circa 1930s. *Courtesy Gray Historical Society*

Left: White's Bridge area, Windham, circa 1936. *Courtesy Windham Historical Society*

Right: Aerial view of Cornish, 1936. *Courtesy Portland Press Herald*

Two

Transportation

Judging by the photographs in the following chapter, transportation in and around Maine's western lakes and mountains region was an altogether more genteel, or perhaps only more relaxed affair many decades ago.

Today, it's hard to imagine being able to travel the inland waters all the way from Portland Harbor to Harrison. But via the Cumberland and Oxford Canal – completed in 1830, though never extended into Oxford County as originally planned – one could journey in leisurely fashion the entire distance of as much as 38 miles, from the city to some lakeside inn or resort. The first 20 miles of the route, out through Westbrook to Sebago Lake Basin, constituted the excavated canal; the remainder included Sebago Lake, the Songo River, and Long Lake.

The canal was closed in 1872, but in some respects,

getting from one place to another was easier a century ago, thanks to railroad service; and the evocative photographs here of train stations such as those in South Waterboro, Harrison and Steep Falls suggest to us that even daily travel once had an undeniably picturesque quality. Horse-drawn carriages, and vintage automobiles – such as the 1901 Model A runabout steam car – exude much the same charm, and induce in us a pleasant nostalgia.

Left: Canal boat passing through Songo Locks in Sebago Lake State Park, two miles south of Naples, circa 1939. *Courtesy Standish Historical Society*

Right: Narrow gauge train in Harrison, late 1800s. *Courtesy Harrison Historical Society*

Above: Steamers on Long Lake, Harrison, late 1800s.
Courtesy Harrison Historical Society

Right: The *Mt. Pleasant* at the wharf in Harrison, circa 1875. It was built to replace the *Oriental* that burned at its wharf in Harrison. The *Mt. Pleasant* was condemned as unseaworthy, circa 1892. *Courtesy Harrison Historical Society*

Above: Gray Depot was established after 1870 with a siding, an express office, a freight shed and a water tower after Maine Central Railroad went through East Gray in 1870. A telegraph station was opened in 1877. It was a better way for Gray people to move their commodities to the cities than by horse-drawn vehicles over the roads. Photo taken in the 1890s. *Courtesy Gray Historical Society*

Left: Miss Mills and her dog out for an afternoon drive in a horse-drawn buggy, Limerick, late 1800s. *Courtesy Sanford Historical Committee*

Above: Philpot's delivery wagon, Limerick, late 1800s. *Courtesy Sanford Historical Committee*

Right: J. Alonzo Fields' stagecoach, Windham. *Courtesy Windham Historical Society*

Above: Digging out the Narrow Gauge Railroad near Harrison, early 1900s. Those known are Clarence Ward, George Lemag and Augustus Bole. *Courtesy Harrison Historical Society*

Above left: Narrow gauge train at the Harrison station, early 1900s.
Courtesy Harrison Historical Society

Left: Narrow gauge train at Harrison Station, early 1900s. *Courtesy Harrison Historical Society*

Transportation

Above: Snow roller in front of Dave Greene and Henry Purington's house on Front Street, Harrison, early 1900s. *Courtesy Harrison Historical Society*

Right: Loren J. Olney in a horse-drawn carriage. He is outside a neighbor's home by Jonello Cottage on the Lower Bay of Kezar Lake. *Courtesy Fryeburg Historical Society*

Above: Automobile, circa 1900, with passengers, presumably friends or relatives of Loren J. Olney, photographer. *Courtesy Fryeburg Historical Society*

Left: This is a photograph of Weston's Covered Bridge before it was rebuilt. *Courtesy Fryeburg Historical Society*

Left: Charles and Frances (Mason) Moulton with their daughter, Olga, being chauffeured by Fred Pierce, Limerick, 1901. *Courtesy Sanford Historical Committee*

Right: Frank York is transporting tourists for Anson Brackett in this horse-drawn wagon, Sebago, early 1900s. *Courtesy Sebago Historical Society*

Below: Israel Lord and his horse, Acton, early 1900s. *Courtesy Sanford Historical Committee*

Above: Model A Runabout, a 1901 steamcar made in Geneva, Ohio. It had self-generating bicycle lights in front. This photo was taken in Sebago, circa 1901. *Courtesy Sebago Historical Society*

Right: South Waterboro Railroad Station, early 1900s.
Courtesy Sanford Historical Committee

Above: Railroad station, Harrison, early 1900s. *Courtesy Harrison Historical Society*

Right: Steep Falls railroad station, circa 1905. *Courtesy Standish Historical Society*

Above: Oxen in road with Julia Rogers, her father, Linwood, and brother Maurice.
Courtesy Windham Historical Society

Right: Horse-drawn grader by the Haley residence in Convene.
Courtesy Sebago Historical Society

Left: The members of the power crew who installed wires for the Portland-Lewiston Interurban electric railroad, Gray, circa 1910. *Courtesy Gray Historical Society*

Right: On August 18, 1914, the Portland-Lewiston Interurban electric railroad had its most distinguished passenger, former president Theodore Roosevelt. "Teddy" is at the rear door addressing a gathering in Gray at the sub-station. This new railroad made commuting to Portland and Lewiston practicable and feasible for the townspeople because the Portland-Lewiston Interurban ran hourly from 7 a.m. to midnight. *Courtesy Gray Historical Society*

Above: Motor coach at John Doherty's stable, Main Street, South Windham. *Courtesy Windham Historical Society*

Left: Horse-drawn buggy in front of Larrabee Farm, North Sebago, circa 1911. *Courtesy Sebago Historical Society*

Above: Road-graders in front of Larrabee home, North Sebago. *Courtesy Sebago Historical Society*

Right: Loren Olney married Ella Weeks of Fryeburg, and lived at 12 Warren Street. He was a photographer and a blacksmith. This photograph shows him in a sleigh outside his home on Warren Street around 1915. *Courtesy Fryeburg Historical Society*

Above: Narrow gauge train in Harrison, circa 1915. *Courtesy Harrison Historical Society*

Left: In front of Howard Blake's home on Ossipee Trail, driver Lin Pitts, lawyer John Hill, Esther (Webster) Blake and others are headed out for a drive. *Courtesy Limington Historical Society*

Transportation

Right: Tourist boat *Songo* provided transportation between Sebago Lake, Songo River and Naples. Photo, circa 1937.
Courtesy Maine Historic Preservation Commission

Below: Railroad workers in Standish, circa 1910. Will Meserve is pictured on the left.
Courtesy Standish Historical Society

Above: One of the trolley cars of the Portland-Lewiston Interurban electric railroad that served Gray. The cars featured mahogany interiors, bronze metalwork, and green plush seats. The cars were named for flowers, such as "Narcissus". The first run was in 1913 and the last run was in 1933. Photo circa 1920. *Courtesy Gray Historical Society*

Three

Schools & Education

Schooldays, schooldays ... If the photographs in the chapter that follows are anything to go by, education appears to have been a much more formal affair, and an altogether more serious one, around the turn of the 20th century.

You have to look carefully to spot a smile, or even an animated expression, on the faces of these young scholars. Could that be the beginnings of a grin on the features of Harry McKeen in the 1913 West Fryeburg School House photo? Is that a smile, or a grimace, exhibited by the young man third from the right outside the Old Town Hall school in Windham in 1910?

One also wonders why, in contrast to those in virtually all class portraits, this schoolyard group is not squeezed ("move closer together, please!") into neat rows, massed together like the entire – and often barefoot – Fryeburg Grammar School 1912-13 population. Were the Windham children interrupted during their recess, perhaps? Only when we examine the chapter's photographs of athletic teams do we see smiles begin to appear with more regularity, as with the Bridgton Academy girls' basketball team of 1935. Equally fascinating are the team uniforms, and footwear, of yesteryear.

Left: Potter Academy class of 1925, Sebago Center. Pictured from left are Martha Robinson, Merle Douglass, Arnold Ward and Dennis McKenney. *Courtesy Sebago Historical Society*

Right: East Sebago School children, 1891. Bert Jewell was the teacher.
Courtesy Sebago Historical Society

Above: Fryeburg Grammar School students, June 1892. Pictured are, Martha Abbot Turner, Clara Tarbox, Ruth Lee Glines, Alice Chase, Clara Page, Sadie Glines, Lena Howe Smith, Martha Chase, and Rachel Weston. *Courtesy Fryeburg Historical Society*

Above: Pennell Institute is one of the most highly styled Italianate high school buildings in Maine, built in 1876, and the Science Laboratory, 1897, at a cost of $21,300. The school was considered one of the finest free high schools of its kind in all of New England. The building was donated by Henry Pennell to the Town of Gray for the sole purpose of education. Pennell Institute is now on the National Register of Historic Places.
Courtesy Gray Historical Society

Right: Limerick Summer School students pose for this photo in front of Town Hall in Limerick, circa 1894.
Courtesy Sanford Historical Committee

Above: Potter Academy students perform "My Brother's Keeper," Sebago Center, 1896. Performers are: Geo. H. Rounds, Lizzie M. Jewell, Limuel Rich, Emma Clough, Will I. Rand, Montford P. Fitch, Edna Dyer, Herbert Thompson. *Courtesy Sebago Historical Society*

Above: South Harrison School students inside their school, circa 1895. Pictured, front to back, first row: Minta Strout and Susie Strout. Second row: Rena Buck, Myrtle Batchelder and Gertrude Pendexter. Third row: Ella Thomspon, Isabel Spaulding and Geneva Merrow. Fourth row: Zilla Fogg, Bertha Strout, Lutie Buck and Teacher Sarah Milliken. Fifth row: Allie Pendexter, Ruth Buck and Ethel Pendexter. Sixth row: Percy Buck, Perley Batchelder and Carroll Strout. Seventh row: George Buck and Prentiss Fogg.
Courtesy Harrison Historical Society

Right: Standish School House and campus, late 1800s.
Courtesy Standish Historical Society

Above: Windham High School class of 1898. The class included Jesse Howard Ayer, Marcia Ella Elder, Lincoln Everett Hall, Arthur Howard Harmon, William Cuyler Hawkes, Marion Redfield Jordan, Grace Viola Lamb, Mabel Elizabeth Lamb, Addie LeGrow, Wesley Mayberry McLellan, Mary Jane Morrell, Harry B. Philpot, Lionel Hersey Pride, and Maude May Varney. *Courtesy Windham Historical Society*

Above: Boulter School spring term, Standish, 1898. Included in the photo are Susie Chick, Norris Berry, Grover Libby, Rudie Burnham, Sonnie Bernham, Hattie Merserve, Millard Boulter, Johnnie Boulter, and Roy Boulter. *Courtesy Standish Historical Society*

Left: Winter in the 1890s was problematic for school attendance. Conveyance for children living in remote areas was required by a state law. As many as four other school districts with fewer children would merge at the Franklin School, North Limington, during the winter months. One Limington resident recalls attending Franklin in the 1940s when there were eight grades in that one school. *Courtesy Limington Historical Society*

Left: Maple Ridge School, Harrison, early 1900s.
Courtesy Harrison Historical Society

Below left: This is a photograph of teacher Edith Farmington Charles with her students. They are standing in front of the Fryeburg Center School.
Courtesy Fryeburg Historical Society

Below: The Village School, circa 1900, which is now the Fryeburg Public Library. *Courtesy Fryeburg Historical Society*

Above: Potter Academy, Sebago Center, early 1900s.
Courtesy Sebago Historical Society

Right: Standish High School graduating class, 1901. Pictured, left to right, back row: Principal Fred Hill, Thomas A. Wingate, Herbert L. Chaplin, Harvey Richardson, E. Henry Mitchell, Chester Milliken, Ralph Richardson, Jessie Dorset, Osborne Riley, James Ridlon and Sherman Hoyt. Second row: Miss Mary Rand (teacher), Bertha Buzzell, Eva Murch, Mollie Freeman Richardson, Eunice Emery Mayo, Gertrude Bean Rand, Bessie Chadbourne Keller and Eva Nason Coolbroth. Front row: Elizabeth Dyer Black, Susie Thombs, Margaret Chick Dorsett, Lillian White Norton, Maude Paine Hill and Edwina Fuller Damme. *Courtesy Standish Historical Society*

Above: Oak Hill School students, Standish, 1901. Front row: Leland Whitney, Harland Moody, Neal Wheeler, Walter Swartz, Harold Rand, Lenny Rand, and Fred Paine. Middle row: Vesta Rand, Ola Cram, Mildred Alley, Edna Whitney, Meede Dolloff, Myrtle Moody, Vera Paine, Floris Whitney, Elsie Libby, Gertrude Rand (teacher), and Edith Wheeler. Back row: Viola Rand, Bertha Stearns, Rob Moody, Ralph Moody, Wilfred Paine, and Clifford Fogg.
Courtesy Standish Historical Society

Left: In 1886 the first classes began at Pennell Institute. Students of Gray along with students from nearby towns who didn't have a high school attended. The first class graduated in 1889. Photo circa 1903.
Courtesy Gray Historical Society

Below: Harrison Grammar School students. Pictured, front row are: Wilma Southworth, Blanche Wood, Arthur Smith, Lester Caswell, Dean Martin, Merle Whitney, Laurence Sylvester, Annie Purington, Esma Hutchins and Ruth Sylvester. The back row includes Harrington Flint, Ray Lamb, Carroll Ward, Teacher Etta Lamb, Ethel Haskell, Percy Martin, Fred Wood, Cecil Nevers, Freda Hapgood, Percy Smith, and Carrie Whitney.
Courtesy Harrison Historical Society

Above: Old Brick School at Windham Center, circa 1900. Pictured are Teacher Edith Pride Elliot with Ethel Swett Burgess, Maurice Rogers, Gertrude Loviett Burnell, Roland Sayward (barefoot), Horace Sayward, Burleigh Loviett, Edna Hawkes, Ethel Allen, Louie Holt and Christine Loviett. *Courtesy Windham Historical Society*

Above: Windham High School students, 1909. Classes were held in Town Hall. *Courtesy Windham Historical Society*

Below: Class of 1906 graduating from Pennell Institute at Gray. Left to right: Frank Merrill, Leroy Libby, Harold Clapp, Ralph Dow, Fred Webb, Mildred Colley, Ethel Whitney, Irene Foster, Grace Doughty, and Edith Fogg. *Courtesy Gray Historical Society*

Above: Standish High School, early 1900s. This building is now Schoolhouse Arts Center in Sebago Lake Village. *Courtesy Standish Historical Society*

Right: Old Brick School at Windham Center. *Courtesy Windham Historical Society*

Above: School at the Old Town Hall, Windham, 1910. Students include Edith Rogers, Mabel Greenlaw, Elizabeth Strout, Carolyn Strout, Bertha and Bernice Sawyer (twins), Marion Greenlaw, Lawrence Rogers, and Percy Rogers. Carolyn Nash was the teacher. *Courtesy Windham Historical Society*

Right: The entire Fryeburg Grammar School for the school year of 1912-1913. Back row: Loring Howe, Alfred Snow, James Kiesman, Merele Abbott, Flora Ela, Myrtle Ballard, Mildred Nelson, Lenora Files (Teacher), Gertrude Johnson, Abbot Smith (Teacher), Helen Haley, Abby Ballard (Teacher), Verna Howe, Roy Abbott, Roland RIchardson, Lyman Ela, Robert Richardson, John Sargent, Warren Haley. Second row: Eliza Watson, Edna Colby, Clifford Eastman, Gerry Cousins, Frances Kenerson, Gwendolyn Brackett, Johnny Snow, Doris Ballard, Eleanor Page, John Potter, Brewster Page, Wellington Porter, Myron Keefe. Third row: Ruth Gaffner, Lillian Shaw, Arthur Hodgson, Olive Ballard, Dorothy Howe, Eleanor Kerr, Geraldine Mason, Eulia Lord, Helen Sargent, Wright Cousins, Albert Ridlon, James Osgood, Harold Kiesman, Chester Ela. Front row: Clifford Gray, Willis Potter, Robert Eastman, Ronald Watson, Clayton Osgood, Grand Hodgdon, Ted Nicholson, Harold Potter, Bernard Howe, Clarence Potter, Perley Snow, Frank Ballard, Roger Ballard, Chester Keefe, Clifford Hill.   *Courtesy Fryeburg Historical Society*

Below: Anderson School on River Road near the Westbrook line, Windham, early 1900s. This school was established in 1770 and was closed in 1934.
Courtesy Windham Historical Society

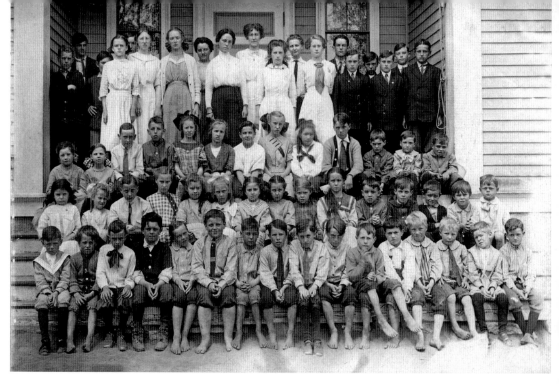

Above: Bernard James McGraw was the coach of this Hebron Academy track team, 1910.   *Courtesy Priscilla Hickey*

Right: This is a photograph of a teacher and her schoolchildren in 1913 at the West Fryeburg School House, located on the side toward Ralph Hill. From left to right, bottom row: Harry McKeen, Carrol Thompson, Chester Heath, Daniel Hutchins, Charlie McKeen, Floyd Stevens and Donald McKeen; second row: Ruth Coleman, Lillian Stevens, Rachel Martin, Ariel McIntire, Leena McIntire, Helen Hutchins and Alice Ballard; third row: Mary Hutchins, Ethel Andrews, Mildred Thompson, Harold Gingell, Kate McIntire and Henry McIntire; fourth row: Hazel Seavey, Sarah Hutchins, Bessie Morrison, Mildred Seavey, Louis Coleman and Byron Hutchins.   *Courtesy Fryeburg Historical Society*

Above: Waterboro High School graduates, 1913. *Courtesy Sanford Historical Committee*

Right: Bridgton Academy boys' basketball team, 1919. In the photo are Ralph Wentworth, Carlton Linscott, Earlon Abbott, Leonard Carsley, Herbert Adams, Herbert Moulton and teacher Charles Rowe. *Courtesy Harrison Historical Society*

Above: Potter Academy boys' basketball team, Sebago Center, 1914. Standing are Guy Philbrook, Irving Philbrook, Archie Shaw. Sitting: Floyd Wentworth, Roy Archibald and Roy Meserve. *Courtesy Sebago Historical Society*

Right: Pennell Institute Baseball Team, Gray, 1920. First row: Egbert Andrews, Guy Prince, Percy Quint and Byron Hanson. Second row: Dana McConkey, Charles Campbell, Anderson Merrill, Edward Kent and Chester Campbell. Third Row: Joseph Leonard, Merton Sweetser, and John Andrews. Fourth row: Teachers Annie Bailey, Susie Wentworth, N. C. Smart and Earl R. Steeves. *Courtesy Gray Historical Society*

Above: The students of the Fryeburg Grammar School, circa 1921. *Courtesy Fryeburg Historical Society*

Right: Bridgton Academy, 1922. Pictured, front row are Evelyn Evans, Frances Tufts, Elaine Rankin, Edna Fogg, Frances Hebb and Lida Harmon. Middle row: Walker Abbott, Ralph Stearns, Clarence Packard, Paul Walker, Francis Berry, Henry Lynch, Eddie Wall and George Crockett. Back row: Raymond Kimball, Wade Hapgood, Leonard Carsley. *Courtesy Harrison Historical Society*

Below: Northeast Field Student Conference at Camp Maqua in Poland, circa 1921. Students came from more than ten schools in three states, including Bates, Colby and Boston University. *Courtesy Isabel Lewando*

Above: New Gloucester High School students in 1923. *Courtesy Maine State Museum*

Above: Windham High School students, 1923. From left, front row: Mildred Plummer, Gladys Rogers, Norma Rogers, Abbie Muzzey, Annie Hall, Doris Allen, Edna Merrill, Annie Rogers, and Alice Libby. Second row: Reginald Bacon, Clifford Morrill, Clifton Reeves, Dana Parsons, Norman Hill, Donald Manson, Robert Trickey, Alice Haskell, Virginia Lord, Annie Freeman, Alma Manchester, Marion Crockett, and Josephine Manchester. Third row: Earl Anderson (in front of Cedric), Cynthia McLellan, _____ Hawkes, Oweena Sylvester, Marjorie Loviett, Ruth Seavey, Helena Libby, Leonard Freeman, Ralph Perkins, unidentified, Horace McLellan, Elmer Gates, Carolyn Strout, and Percy Fogg. Fourth row: Cedric Foster, Edward Knowles, Howard Rogers, Prescott Murphy, David Taylor, Lyle Cook, William McPhee, and Edith McKenzie. Fifth row: Inez Westcott, Frances Fogg, Florence Ward, Doris Borge, Lillian Lamb, Louise Kennard, _____ Morrill, Gladys Foye, and Hazel Greenlaw. Back row: Lyndon Rogers, Horace Smith, Charles Legrow, Norman Tozier (teacher), unidentified, Myra Thurlow (teacher), John Hall, Priscilla Bishop (teacher), unidentified, Harold Cobb (principal), Merton Gates, and John Nash. *Courtesy Windham Historical Society*

Right: Senior Class of 1922. Back row, from left: Lillian Swan, Robert Eastman, Miss Ethel Cooley, coach, LaForrest Horton, Howard Bean, Eldred Littlefield. Front row: Doris Chandler, Merwin Woodward, Eula Lord, Francis Buzzell, Robert Moulton, Norman Kendall. *Courtesy Fryeburg Historical Society*

Above: Black and white photograph of students and their teacher Miss Ellis at the C.A. Snow School, 1923. This building now serves as the administrative offices for School Administrative District 72. Those known, first row: Frances Shaw, Clyde ____, Vera Haley, Raymond Drowns, Ernest Mills, Ellen Wiley, Aubrey Keefe, Lottie Drowns, Wilfred Springer, John Pike, Dorothy Craig, Althea Lord, John Stearns, Edward Mills, ____Potter, Walter Drowns, Barbara Buzzell, John Black , Jack Jordon, Howard Potter, Doris Potter, Audrey Pendexter, Mary Leadbeater, Carl Johnson, Esther Pike, Clyde Johnson, Ruth Mills, Ridgerly Kiesman, Charles Thurlow and Lawrence Whiting. Second row: Esther Peterson Allen, Ruth Wiley O'Connor, Leon (Pete) Ballard, Harold Thomas, Kenneth Howard, Loring Hurd, John Thurlow, Gladys Marston Leach, Thelma Rogers, Howard Kiesman, Alice Rogers, Billy Craig, Florence Stevens, Hazel Haley Tarbox, Doris Haley, Lilian Haley McAllister, Irene Hamilton, Pauline Perham, Lucy Buzzell, Thelma Rogers, Rebecca Johnson, Roger Burnell, Thelma Lord, Eleanor Goodridge, Phyllis Marston, Shirley Gaffner, Leona Kiesman Dennison, Edmund Emerson, Dudley Perkins and Alden Lord. Third row: Pearl Mills, Helen Ballard, Eleanor Lord, Phillip Watson, James Merrill, Esther Gaffner, Bertha Rogers, Leah McIntyre Irish, Dorothy Potter, Ruth Jenness, Annie Bemis, Belyea, Nettie Keefe, Asa Osgod Pike, Virgil Kiesman, Louis Solari, Miss Ellis (Teacher), Emily Walker Steadman Philbrook. *Courtesy Fryeburg Historical Society*

Right: Standish High School boys' baseball team, 1925. Pictured, left to right, front row: Lawrence Rand, Raiford Wedge, Chas. Watson, Charles Graffam, and Wilson Hawkes. Back row: Kenneth Moore, Kenneth Chaplin, Owen Sandborn, Mr. Frank Lewis, Dr. Olin Moulton, Warren Rand and Skinner Libby. *Courtesy Standish Historical Society*

Right: Standish High School boys' basketball team, 1927. Pictured, first row: Ned Dolloff, Charles Graffam, Lawrence Rand. Second row: Wilbur Sanborn, Alden Shaw. Standing alone at the top of the stairs is Clyde Dolloff.
Courtesy Standish Historical Society

Below: Potter Academy, class of 1927, Sebago Center. Pictured, first row are Elizabeth Nason Getchell, Linwood Merrifield, Marion Dolloff Nason, Guy Ridlon and Edna Douglass Hale. Back row: Doris Weed Douglass, Eula Larabee Lewis, Everett Chadbourne, Kenneth Ridlon, Doris Dolloff Hamilton and Marion Ward Graffam.
Courtesy Sebago Historical Society

Above: Harrison Intermediate School children, circa 1928. Pictured, first row are Arne Nummela, Jim Williamson, Paul Poikonen, Vernon Brown, Edward Martin, Gerald Haley, Kenneth Chapman, Stanley Freeman and Lawrence St. John. Second row: Teacher Beatrice Wyman, Alice Martin, Ellen Harney, Elma Anderson, Alberta Nason, Marcia Walker, Geraldine Harmon, Martha Stuart and Annette Hunter. Third row: Ronell Fleck, Harry Winslow, Oscar Anderson, Robert Higgins, Wesley Tenney, Sherman Flock, Duane Bedell, Robert Clemmons, Kenneth Packard and Burton St. John. *Courtesy Harrison Historical Society*

Above: Potter Academy girls' basketball team, 1930-31, Sebago. Pictured, front row are Lucretia Decker, Edith Robinson, Belle Hall, Dot Merrifield, Elizabeth Durrell and Dolly Dolloff. Back row: Coach Harold Dodge, Olive Dolloff, Elizabeth Trumble, Eleanor Thombs, Rachel Brown, and Arline Burnell.
Courtesy Sebago Historical Society

Right: Standish High School students, 1929.
Courtesy Standish Historical Society

Above: Bridgton Academy girls' basketball team, 1935. Pictured, front row, are Coach Lillian Hanscom, Edna Brett, Thelma Edes, Mabelle Hersey, Helen Martikainen, Florence Spaulding, Mary McIntire, Maida Chapman and assistant coach Ruth Rounds. Back row: May Lundstrom, Irja Martikainen, Geraldine Harmon, Emma Libby, Madelyn Buck and Virginia Tyler. *Courtesy Harrison Historical Society*

Right: The Standish High School boys' basketball team of 1936 won the Gorham Normal School Tournament. Pictured, left to right, front row: E. Ettinger, C. Snowden, N. Carver, R. Austin and W. Witham. Back row: Coach Johnson, P. Rand, R. Edgecomb, B. Graffam, and E. Hubbard (manager). *Courtesy Standish Historical Society*

Above: Windham High School Home economics class, circa 1939. The teacher, Sarah McComb is holding the banner. *Courtesy Windham Historical Society*

Left: Standish High School, Triple C Championship baseball team, 1937. Pictured, left to right, front row: R. Wood, N. Carver, R. Graffam, R. Edgecomb, W. Witham, and G. Decker. Back row: R. Dole, L. Paine, R. Austin, C. Woodbrey, G. Boothby, G. Libby (manager), and Coach Johnson. *Courtesy Standish Historical Society*

Four

Commerce & Industry

With this chapter, we roll along with the busy wheels of commerce through the decades from 1879 to the years shortly before World War II. These photographs capture the breadth of the lakes-and-mountains-region's commercial and industrial undertakings. Woolen mills, and factories, such as canning and chair-manufacturing; blacksmith shops and banks; and a wide range of retail operations, from George Bowden's handsome ice cream stand in Shapleigh, to the D.M. Rand Apothecary in South Windham, to the H.H. Caswell Grocery Store, built in 1892, in Harrison.

Lumber, of course, has been among Maine's foremost industries since the arrival of the first European settlers, and in these pages we visit sawmills, pulp and paper mills and even remote logging camps. Indeed, haulers and their teams of horses – for example, in the century-old pictures from Pine Grove camp in Norway – provide the subjects of some of the most absorbing portraits here.

As hospitality and tourism have ever been a hallmark of the region, here too are inns and hotels, their chefs and waitresses, and a boarding house with its "table girls." Even the garages, gas stations and automobiles, here seen beginning to transform the face of our main streets, manifest the charm of another era.

Left: Many farmers in Gray grew corn, and it was one of the most profitable field crops. The first canning factory opened in 1887. Left to right: Roy McDonald, Carl Woodbury, Harold Clapp, Susie Stiles Hanson, Ethel Stiles, unknown, and Raymond Libby. Photo early 1900s. *Courtesy Gray Historical Society*

Right: Men and horse-drawn wagons pose in front of J.L. Illsley's on Main Street in Harrison, circa 1879. Illsley sold his business in 1880. *Courtesy Harrison Historical Society*

Above: In 1836 the Oxford Bank in Fryeburg was organized, but never actually opened for business. In 1839 an attempt was made in Portland to float notes from this non-functioning institution as part of a swindling scheme. This is an example of one of those notes. On the face of the bill the god of commerce and wealth, Mercury, is watching over the business. *Courtesy Fryeburg Historical Society*

Above: Mayall Mills at North Gray was the first water-powered woolen mill in the United States. Samuel Mayall was processing wool in Gray by 1791. In 1806 he advertised new, faster machinery and added a dyeing operation to the carding, spinning, weaving and fulling processes. After his death in 1831 the family leased the mill to a series of managers, and later sold to William Beatty, who continued to operate in the building. Today, the site, with its crumbling bricks and granite stones is a landmark that has been preserved by the State of Maine and several groups as a park. *Courtesy Gray Historical Society*

Left: Chair factory, before it burned in Harrison in 1907. *Courtesy Harrison Historical Society*

Above: Logging camp and sawmill with oxen team, horse teams, lumber piles and teamsters, West Paris, circa 1880s. *Courtesy Maine State Museum*

Above: Jordan and Emery coat shop, Harrison, late 1800s. The long, covered walkway was later removed. Freeland H. Ricker bought the coat shop building and fitted it for a grocery and hardware store, moving his business into it from the corner store on Front Street. He continued to operate his store at this location until the 1907 fire destroyed the building and nearly all the contents. He immediately began the construction of a new building and moved into it five months later. *Courtesy Harrison Historical Society*

Left: Gray's largest merchandising store, Hancock & Company, was built in 1876 by Henry Goff from the bricks of his own brickyard. A wooden horse shed and grain house was attached at the back of the store. The third floor was used by the Odd Fellows organization. Several other businesses have occupied this store. The team of horses at the right belonged to Orville Hanson. The building burned in the big fire of 1920. Photo circa 1890. *Courtesy Gray Historical Society*

Above: Bicyclists line up in front of F.H. Townsend's store, Limerick, early 1900s.
Courtesy Sanford Historical Committee

Right: W. Adams & Son store on Main Street, Limerick, early 1900s. *Courtesy Sanford Historical Committee*

Above: Blacksmith Shop on the ridge (Hancock Pond Road), West Sebago, early 1900s. It was later owned and operated by Louis Chessey from 1925 until his retirement. *Courtesy Sebago Historical Society*

Left: Limerick Mills Boarding House, circa 1900.
Courtesy Sanford Historical Committee

Above: Original Hartford Coat Shop, early 1900s. Hartford was the owner of the first telephone company in Standish.
Courtesy Standish Historical Society

Left: Guests at Chaddurne Cottage, Sebago, circa 1900. *Courtesy Sebago Historical Society*

Above: E.W. Dolloff Store, owned by Edward Dolloff, Standish Corner, early 1900s.
Courtesy Standish Historical Society

Left: Smith's Mills sawmill crew, Standish, early 1900s.
Courtesy Standish Historical Society

Left: Two men hauling logs with a horse team in the Fryeburg area, early 1900s.
Courtesy Fryeburg Historical Society

Above: A 100-room, turn-of-the-19th century inn located on Main Street in Fryeburg. This was a popular summer tourist destination for visitors to the Mount Washington Valley. It was destroyed by fire in 1906.
Courtesy Fryeburg Historical Society

Right: Bonny Eagle Post Office, early 1900s. *Courtesy Standish Historical Society*

Above: Sawmill at Douglasville, which was located at the head of Little Sebago Lake. Photo circa 1900. *Courtesy Gray Historical Society*

Below: Harrison House, Harrison, circa 1905. *Courtesy Harrison Historical Society*

Above: F.H. Townsend's store, early 1900s. In the car the man in the back seat on the right is Fred H. Townsend. Dora Townsend can be seen wearing a white blouse, and standing next to her is Mattie Mason. This was the second car in Limerick. *Courtesy Sanford Historical Committee*

Left: Interior of the Hartford Coat Shop, Standish, early 1900s. *Courtesy Standish Historical Society*

Right: Harry Fitch's sawmill in East Sebago. The Chilton Paint Co. advertisement was paid for by the Chilton Co. as was advertising space on barns and roofs across the country.
Courtesy Sebago Historical Society

Left: Corn factory workers pose for a photograph, South Waterboro, early 1900s. *Courtesy Sanford Historical Committee*

Above: Folks gather outside a store in South Waterboro, circa 1905.
Courtesy Sanford Historical Committee

Left: The D.M. Rand Apothecary in South Windham, circa 1905.
Courtesy Collections of the Warren Memorial Library

Above: A skoot (sled) is shown behind a team of oxen in the Limington area. These were used to pull very heavy loads. *Courtesy Limington Historical Society*

Left: This image of an ox team hauling logs was shot by world-renowned photographer William B. Post. Post moved to Fryeburg in 1901 and married Mary Webster Weston. They lived at the Fryeburg Tavern, where the local fire station now stands.
Courtesy Fryeburg Historical Society

Below: The L.S. Patch General Store and post office in Shapleigh, circa 1909. Leroy S. Patch, the man with the derby, standing by the door, operated the store from the late 1800s until the 1940s. He also served as Shapleigh's postmaster from about 1896 to early in 1940.
Courtesy Sanford Historical Committee

Above: Picking apples at C.S. Phinney Orchards in Standish, 1907. Charles Chase, Civil War Veteran, is the only one identified, and he is pictured on the left. *Courtesy Standish Historical Society*

Above: Fred S. Hawkes' store at Windham Center. The school was located on the second floor in 1907. *Courtesy Windham Historical Society*

Right: Interior of Fred Hawkes' Store, Windham Center, circa 1907.
Courtesy Windham Historical Society

Above: H.H. Boody dry goods store at North Windham Corner, early 1900s.
Courtesy Windham Historical Society

Left: Grain store across from Hawkes', Windham Center.
Courtesy Windham Historical Society

Left: Hauling logs near the Pine Grove logging camp, Norway, circa 1905. Included in the photo are teamster Will Mortley and owner George H. McKrew. *Courtesy Maine State Museum*

Right: Pine Grove logging camp, Norway, circa 1905. Those identified include Will Mortley (far left with dog), Fred McKeen (standing in front of log sled at left), Bertha McKeen (woman at left center with fur coat), Annie Hall (next to Bertha), and Lillian McKeen (little girl in front of tree). *Courtesy Maine State Museum*

Above: Logging crew at Douglas Hill, Sebago, circa 1913. *Courtesy Sebago Historical Society*

Left: George Bowden's ice cream stand, Shapleigh, circa 1912. The stand was located near Crosby's Store on the road to Mousam Lake. The building was later moved to the lake and converted into a cottage. *Courtesy Sanford Historical Committee*

Left: Bridge between Gorham and South Windham, before 1916. Androscoggin Pulp and Paper Mill can be seen at the right. *Courtesy Windham Historical Society*

Right: Trig Tandberg's delivery wagon delivering hay to one of its customers, circa 1917. *Courtesy Kelley Tandberg*

Above: Fryeburg Lumber Company Box Mill, circa 1915. The board yard was the old race track in the gay nineties. *Courtesy Fryeburg Historical Society*

Right: Many Limington men worked for the Androscoggin Pulp Company in Steep Falls across the Saco River from Limington. Left to right: Jerry Kennison, Alonzo Foster, Roscoe Emery, Henry Huard, Albert Strout, Alfred Black, Joe Peters, Jack Guilant, Walter Taylor, Jesse Dorset and Charles York. In 1934, the Cumberland County Power and Light Company bought the buildings of the Pulp Company when it took over the water rights. On November 21, 1935, a fire of undetermined origin destroyed the three large remaining buildings of the mill. *Courtesy Limington Historical Society*

Commerce & Industry

Left: Andrew Johnson (1854-1943) came to Gray as a young lad. He worked for a company in Gray that manufactured sleighs and carriages. He then studied at the Technical School for Carriage and Automobile Draftsmen and Mechanics in New York, and at the Albert DuPont School in Paris. He taught at the New York school, and later in Detroit. In his retirement, he returned to Gray and ran a correspondence school from his residence. He had trained more than 2,500 men, of whom many became giants in the automobile industry. The famous Fisher Brothers were among his students. Andrew was a pioneer of early automobile design. *Courtesy Gray Historical Society*

Right: Table girls (waitresses) at Dyke Mountain Farm, a boarding house at Winn Mountain in Sebago, 1925. *Courtesy Sebago Historical Society*

Above: Woolen Mill at Mallison Falls, 1916. *Courtesy Windham Historical Society*

Right: Charles Dimock joined his father, William, to run the Limington village store in 1877. Mr. Dimock and Gus Black are shown in front of that building, which in later years was the Limington Grange. *Courtesy Limington Historical Society*

Left: Douglas Inn chefs, circa 1925. *Courtesy Sebago Historical Society*

Above: Waitresses at Douglas Inn at Douglas Mountain, circa 1925. *Courtesy Sebago Historical Society*

Right: Douglas Inn, Douglas Mountain, Sebago, 1925. *Courtesy Sebago Historical Society*

Left: Douglas Inn, circa 1925. It was built in 1903 by Edward Douglas at Douglas Mountain in Sebago. The inn would burn in 1928. *Courtesy Sebago Historical Society*

Above: Harrison House, Harrison, circa 1925. It was razed in 1964.
Courtesy Harrison Historical Society

Right: L.M. Sanborn's Store and Post Office, East Sebago, circa 1925.
Courtesy Sebago Historical Society

Above: Elms Inn, Harrison, circa 1928. It was torn down in 2005. *Courtesy Harrison Historical Society*

Above: Lawrence and Leighton Garage was the old livery stable of the Elm House Inn. The garage was opened in the 1920s and operated for several years.
Courtesy Gray Historical Society

Right: The Bean Hole Restaurant, on Route 302 in the Windham area, in 1926, owned by the Lowell family.
Courtesy Windham Historical Society

Above: Len Libby Candies original location, Spurwink Road, Scarborough.
Courtesy Len Libby Candies

Right: Gulf gas station in Standish, circa 1930. It later became S & S Auto Repair.
Courtesy Standish Historical Society

Left: Summit Spring Hotel, Harrison, circa 1933. It burned in 1969.
Courtesy Harrison Historical Society

Above: Dry Mills Store, located in the Dry Mills section of Gray, was a town landmark for many years. There were many storekeepers. Photo 1930s. *Courtesy Gray Historical Society*

Right: Dry Mills mill crew in the winter of 1934-1935. The mill provided employment for many people in the Gray area. *Courtesy Gray Historical Society*

Left: Vehicles at the Gulf Station in Harrison, 1930s. In the photo are a 1931 Dodge, a 1932 Reo, and a 1935 Chevy Hot Dog. *Courtesy Harrison Historical Society*

Above: Grand Union Tea Company delivery wagon, Sebago. *Courtesy Sebago Historical Society*

Right: The Old Mill, Harrison, circa 1939. *Courtesy Harrison Historical Society*

Below: Corn being delivered and dumped at the Burnham & Morrill Canning Factory in Fryeburg. *Courtesy Fryeburg Historical Society*

Above: This shop was owned by C. T. Ladd and located on Portland Street in Fryeburg. This photograph was taken in 1937.
Courtesy Fryeburg Historical Society

Below: Chocolate hand-dipper at Len Libby Candies in the early days. *Courtesy Len Libby Candies*

Five

Recreation

It is generally held to be true that people of several generations ago worked longer days and had less leisure time than we are accustomed to. Yet the photographs that follow make clear that our forebears really knew how to enjoy themselves. Indoors, dances, held at halls such as the pavilion at Sebago Lake Station, were wildly popular; people were accustomed to making their own fun, as in the intense card game shown here, from 1896. And as often as weather permitted, folks availed themselves of the recreational opportunities in which western Maine is so uniquely rich.

Camping, hunting, fishing, swimming; engaged in team sports, riding a carousel, or savoring a day at the county fair race track; sailing, skating, skiing ... the list is nearly endless. One of the most charming photographs here is surely that of the July 4, 1894 picnic party near White's Bridge in Standish – note the costumes and the festive gaiety of the ladies' parasols. One of the most amusing may be that of the highly untraditional modified canoe launch about to take place at Camp Ettowah on Kimball Pond. We may also be struck by the fairly formal dress of people ostensibly out to have a good time – few of us today would wear a tie on a fishing expedition.

Left: Outing on Mousam Lake, near the G.A.R. camp, Shapleigh, early 1900. Weekly rent in 1910 for a camp that would sleep up to ten was $10.50, with everything furnished except linens. Even a rowboat came with the deal. The G.A.R. Camps had no affiliation with the Civil War veterans organization. The letters are said to have stood for Grand Army Review at first and later for Great American Republic. *Photo courtesy Sanford Historical Committee, text by Harland H. Eastman*

Right: Howard McDonald, a magician, gives a performance in Standish, late 1800s. He died in 1930 and is buried in Harding Cemetery. *Courtesy Standish Historical Society*

Above: Judge's stand at the "old" Fryeburg Fair, prior to 1885. The Fryeburg Fair was organized in 1851 by Peleg Wadsworth, Samuel Stickney, E.L. Osgood and John W. Dana, who formed the West Oxford Agricultural Society. For the first seven years the West Oxford Agricultural Society's fair location rotated to the towns included in the West Oxford area: Fryeburg, Brownfield, Porter, Denmark and Lovell. On October 6, 1885, the Society bought the present-day Fryeburg Fairgrounds and from then on, the fair has been held in Fryeburg. *Courtesy Fryeburg Historical Society*

Below: Pavilion at Sebago Lake Station, 1890s. This well-known dance hall was the place to be every weekend. *Courtesy Standish Historical Society*

Above: A card game is enjoyed at the Davis Ranch, Standish, May 27, 1896.
Courtesy Standish Historical Society

Above left: A day at the beach in the late 1800s.
Courtesy Standish Historical Society

Left: Steamboat outing on Mousam Lake, circa 1900.
Courtesy Sanford Historical Committee

Above: Three fishermen display their catch in Sebago, circa 1900.
Courtesy Sebago Historical Society

Right: Four fishermen at a camp in the lakes region, circa 1900.
Courtesy Sanford Historical Committee

Above: "The dance hall at the G.A.R. camps, Mousam Lake, Shapleigh, early 1900s. In 1896, A.J. Lerned, from Lawrence, Massachusetts, bought land on the eastern shore of Mousam Lake and commenced building camps for summer visitors. Eventually there were 14, all but one named for a Civil War general, the exception being the Admiral Dewey. Among the generals honored were Miles, Sheriden, Grant, Hooker, Butler, Banks, Anderson, Needham and Sampson. ... From 1917 they were owned by Charles Meader, who first worked at the camps for Lerned in 1907." *Photo courtesy Sanford Historical Committee, text quoted from A Cluster of Maine Villages: Sanford and Springvale, Acton, Shapleigh and Alfred, 1991 by Harland Eastman*

Right: John Healy and Charles Bigelow brought a band of "full-blooded Kickapoo Indians" (Sioux, Pawnee, Mohawk, Iroquois and Blackhawk) to the Fryeburg Fair circa 1900 to put on a medicine show to sell Kickapoo Indian Remedies. Their remedies were considered "authentic" because they used herbs and not adulterated alcohol as some remedies did.
Courtesy Fryeburg Historical Society

Above: Image of the cattle barns and the ox teams at the Fryeburg fair, circa 1900. *Courtesy Fryeburg Historical Society*

Left: Horace Day, of Auburn, loved to fish at sporting camps throughout Maine. Photo circa 1910. He was a Lewiston bank president.
Courtesy Anne Farley (MacDonald Family)

Right: "Interior of the Exposition Building, Acton Fair, early 1900s. Built in 1890s, soon after Union Park became the fair's permanent home, the Exposition Building was a landmark for more than 80 years. It housed exhibits of every sort, the fair association's main office and items for sale. The gentlemen in the corner are demonstrating sewing machines. The building burned to the ground early on Saturday morning, August 28, 1976." *Photo courtesy Sanford Historical Committee, text quoted from A Cluster of Maine Villages: Sanford and Springvale, Acton, Shapleigh and Alfred, 1991 by Harland Eastman*

Below: This picture was taken by Fryeburg photographer Loren J. Olney of children cutting ice in Lovell or Fryeburg. *Courtesy Fryeburg Historical Society*

Left: The race is on at Gray Fair Grounds, which was formed in 1885. The half-mile track had a covered grandstand and a judges' stand. The exhibition hall and dining hall were also constructed on the grounds. The Park Association operated the fair until 1902. Photo circa 1900. *Courtesy Gray Historical Society*

Above: Boating on Sebago Lake off Little Indian Island, circa 1905. *Courtesy F.H. Stickney*

Left: "The Broggi Sailboat on Mousam Lake, circa 1904. The young man standing on the super-structure of the boat is Charles Broggi, then a student at Hebron Academy. … Charles was the son of Sanford merchant Frank Broggi and followed his father in the fruit business." *Photo courtesy Sanford Historical Committee, text quoted from Villages on the Mousam, Sanford and Springvale, Maine, 1995 by Harland Eastman*

Above: Quick Lunch Stand at Acton Fair with the Exposition Building which burned in 1976 on the left, circa 1905. *Courtesy Sanford Historical Committee*

Above: Carlton Martin and the black bear he shot in East Sebago, January 13, 1908. The bear weighed 257 pounds. *Courtesy Sebago Historical Society*

Left: The Smart Cottage on Mousam Lake above the G.A.R. Camps, early 1900s. *Courtesy Sanford Historical Committee*

Right: Spaulding families at a camp in the lakes region. The little girls are Rae Spaulding, left and Doris Spaulding, right. Their mother is Francena, and is the second woman from the left. *Courtesy Anne Farley (MacDonald Family)*

Above: Camp Wawenock-Owaissa, South Casco, early 1900s.
Courtesy Maine State Museum

Right: "Ivory H. Fenderson's Carousel at Acton Fair, October 1911. Made by the Armitage-Herschell Company of North Tonawanda, New York, in 1894, this carousel was purchased by Ivory H. Fenderson IV of Saco in 1896 for $2,000. … It is the second oldest carousel in the United States. Mr. Fenderson is on the left in the group of four men standing toward the center. Beside him is Leroy Patch, storekeeper and postmaster at Shapleigh Corner. Alice Patch, Leroy's daughter, is just to the right of the tent pole in a white dress and hat seated on a horse. Others in the photograph, though their order is unknown, are George Muchmore, Katherine Rowell, Beth Murray, Fred Muchmore, Oscar Clark, Lena Ridley, Elsie Austin, George Crediford, Elodia Pray, Bunny Pray, Sadie Pray, Grace Nason, Lora Grant, Bertha Flanders and Dorothy Ridley." *Photo courtesy Sanford Historical Committee, text quoted from A Cluster of Maine Villages: Sanford and Springvale, Acton, Shapleigh and Alfred, 1991 by Harland Eastman*

Above: Newfield baseball field, circa 1915. *Courtesy Sanford Historical Committee*

Left: West Newfield baseball team, circa 1912. *Courtesy Sanford Historical Committee*

Left: "Acton Fair, circa 1915. Harness racing was once a principal attraction at the Acton Fair. … The first Acton Fair was held in 1866 and fairs continued to be held annually up to the 1930s. They alternated between Acton and Shapleigh until 1889 when B.C. and Freeman Jordan gave land near Mousam lake for a permanent location. The new fairgrounds, once called Union Park, opened in October 1890, and has been the site of all fairs since that time. The 1930s and early 1940s were difficult years, and the fair nearly did not survive the Great Depression, and Second World War. It was revived, however, in 1946 by a local organization, now called the York County Agriculture Association, and has been held every year since that time." *Photo courtesy Sanford Historical Committee, text quoted from A Cluster of Maine Villages: Sanford and Springvale, Acton, Shapleigh and Alfred, 1991 by Harland Eastman*

Above: West Shore Camps, operated by Anson Brackett, East Sebago, circa 1920. *Courtesy Sebago Historical Society*

Left: Limerick baseball team, 1911. *Courtesy Sanford Historical Committee*

Above: Horace Day, of Auburn, right, and a companion at a sporting camp in the lakes region, circa 1925. *Courtesy Anne Farley (MacDonald Family*

Right: Arthur N. Bragg (left) and two of his buddies enjoy a day at the lake, circa 1922. *Courtesy Marita Lowell*

Maine Memories

Above: Smelt fishing on Muddy River, Sebago, March 1916. *Courtesy Sebago Historical Society*

Below: Grandstand at North Sebago for a centennial celebration in 1926. *Courtesy Sebago Historical Society*

Above: Sebago town baseball team, circa 1934. Pictured, left to right: Prentiss Wentworth, Melvin Irish, Brick Burnell, John Lord and Linwood Bachilder. Back row: Elwood Edwards, Geo. Fitch, Frank Irish, Ray Burnell, Delma Lord, Floyd Edwards and Bob Gilman.
Courtesy Sebago Historical Society

Left: Years ago, Jockey Cap had a rope tow and was a very popular place to go skiing. This is an image of a skiier at Jockey Cap, circa 1936.
Courtesy Fryeburg Historical Society

Right: This image is of male campers about ready to set off in a canoe. They are at Camp Ettowah, which is located on Kimball Pond in Fryeburg, circa 1934. *Courtesy Fryeburg Historical Society*

Above: Deertrees Theatre in Harrison, circa 1937. *Courtesy Harrison Historical Society*

Left: Aerial view of the Cornish Fair grounds, Cornish 1936. *Courtesy Portland Press Herald*

Above: Trig Tandberg's boat at Sebago Basin, August 1939. *Courtesy Kelley Tandberg*

Right: Trig Tandberg with his catch at Sebago Lake, August 1939. *Courtesy Kelley Tandberg*

Recreation

Above: The "Widderbach," a summer camp belonging to the Prescott family for generations, is located in Ward's Cove on Sebago Lake. "Widderbach" was purchased in 1938 by Doris Prescott and her brother, Clayton McFarland. The camp got its name from Doris being a widow and Clayton being a bachelor. Photo circa 1939. *Courtesy Keely Prescott Cameron*

Above: Thorton Prescott, doing a little yard work at his camp on Sebago Lake, circa 1938. *Courtesy Keely Prescott Cameron*

Right: Doris Prescott, relaxing on the beach in Ward's Cove, on Sebago Lake, circa 1939. *Courtesy Keely Prescott Cameron*

Six

Community

Gathered in groups at their homes or churches, or photographed singly for portraits; assembled behind an itinerant organ-grinder, or enjoying a leisurely game of croquet; posing before libraries, post offices, or in an apple orchard. Here, we may visit the people of a bygone era where they truly lived.

We see them with their pets and livestock (even feeding the hens). We see them at work – farming, picking apples, silhouetted atop an Odd Fellows hall they are building. In some of the most affecting photographs, we see them with their families, as in the well-attended Chase family reunion in Standish a century ago, or the charming vignette in which one Andrew Andersen places a ring upon the finger of Ada, who would become his wife. (It looks as if he has also brought her flowers.)

Another family portrait – of Henry Pitman Waldron and three subsequent generations – gains particular poignance when we note that he and his granddaughter would both die in 1910; he at age 92, she at age 29.

These communities of yesteryear revolved around many things, including churches, farms, town halls, and homesteads. Most of all, we recognize here, those communities were a natural extension of family life.

Left: S.A. Grant residence, Limerick, 1894. *Courtesy Sanford Historical Committee*

Right: In front of this dining hall on Chautauquan grounds is a Chautauquan Circuit. These people were part of a philosophical movement. They would travel all across the country, by a designated Chautauquan Train, to speak to crowds of people. This photograph was taken in the summer of 1889. *Courtesy Fryeburg Historical Society*

Above: Free Will Baptist Church, Windham Center, late 1800s. The church was organized in 1878. *Courtesy Windham Historical Society*

Above: Mary Tarbox Walker is the elderly woman sitting in the back row. Her daughters are Susan, an educator, who died in 1905 (age 78) , Sarah, a home-body, who died at age 38, and sitting left of Mary is Eva, an artist, who died in August 1903 (age 36). Eva was also a teacher in New York prior to returning to Fryeburg at the time of her death. Eva's family lived on Walker Island Farm. *Courtesy Fryeburg Historical Society*

Left: Albion Parris Howe, born in Standish on March 13, 1818. He received an appointment to West Point at the age of 19 at the insistence of the state governor and graduated eighth in a class of 52 in 1841. He was commissioned a second lieutenant in the 4th U.S. Artillery Regiment. He served in the War with Mexico and the Civil War; and fought in the expedition against the Sioux Indians and was a part of John Brown's Raid at Harpers Ferry. He was also Guard of Honor of 12 officers who escorted the remains of President Lincoln from Washington D.C. to Springfield, Missouri. He retired from active service in 1882, and died in 1897. His house was donated to the town and used as a school and later Town Hall and in recent years, Sunrise Corner. *Courtesy Standish Historical Society*

Above: Interior of First Parish Unitarian Church, Standish. The building was constructed in 1805 and is now known as the Old Red Church. *Courtesy Standish Historical Society*

Below: Manchester Family, Windham, 1895. Pictured, front row: Alice, Warren, Ida (mother) and Seward (father), Back row: Everett and Almon. *Courtesy Windham Historical Society*

Above: Residence of Herbert Dow at the corner of Route 35A and Dow Road, Standish, 1890s. Pictured, left to right are Margaret Dow and Harold Dow; in the rocking chair is Almira Dow. Lizzie Dow is wearing a dress by the tree. Vera and Pearle Dow are wearing identical dresses. The man with the horse is Herbert Dow. *Courtesy Standish Historical Society*

Left: Dr. S.C. Buzzell, Standish, late 1800s.
Courtesy Standish Historical Society

Above: Joseph Fogg residence, later Dave Greene's, on Front Street which is now Thomas, Harrison, late 1800s.
Courtesy Harrison Historical Society

Above: Maude Harmon, Standish, late 1800s. *Courtesy Standish Historical Society*

Left: Valentine Carsley's residence in Harrison, late 1800s.
Courtesy Harrison Historical Society

Above: C.S. Phinney home, Standish, late 1800s. *Courtesy Standish Historical Society*

Above: Tolman House in Harrison, late 1800s.
Courtesy Harrison Historical Society

Right: Dr. S.C. Buzzell's residence, Standish, late 1800s. Dr. Buzzell and his family lived here until the 1960s.
Courtesy Standish Historical Society

Above: This was first the Congregational Church, which was built in 1836, and later became the Finnish Lutheran Church, and later the Seventh Day Adventist, Harrison. Photo 1905. *Courtesy Harrison Historical Society*

Left: Homestead of the Manchester family. This 1897 photo includes grandparents, Nahum and Lydia, seated; holding the horse is father Seward; standing, from left is Everett, mother, Ida, and daughter Alice. The baby on the ground at Ida's feet is Warren; Almon is on a hay rake near the wagon by the barn. *Courtesy Windham Historical Society*

Right: Collison children in front of their home on Buxton Road, Route 35, Standish, early 1900s. Buxton Road was renamed Bonny Eagle Road. *Courtesy Standish Historical Society*

Above: Almanzer and Maggie Kallock home, Town Farm and Swett Road. *Courtesy Windham Historical Society*

Right: Original town pump in Standish, looking toward Ossipee Trail East, early 1900s. It was there to provide water for anyone in town who didn't have water. Notice the Lexington Elms still standing at the time of the photo. *Courtesy Standish Historical Society*

Above: The home of Henry B. Hartford was next to his coat shop, Standish, early 1900s. There was also a post office in the coat shop. *Courtesy Standish Historical Society*

Above: Walter Reeves' home on Town Farm Road in Windham, early 1900s. *Courtesy Windham Historical Society*

Right: Walter Davis rolling out the road. The trolley is being pulled by a team of oxen, Standish, early 1900s. Notice the rocks to weigh the roller down. *Courtesy Standish Historical Society*

Left: Hall Homestead, Hall Road, Windham. It was built between 1839 and 1840.
Courtesy Windham Historical Society

Above: Levi Wescott home in Standish near Harding Cemetery, early 1900s.
Courtesy Standish Historical Society

Right: Perley and Florabelle Guptill's house, built in 1875, was next to the Friends' Church on Route 202, Windham. *Courtesy Windham Historical Society*

Maine Memories

Above: Highland Grove, 1920s.
Courtesy Standish Historical Society

Left: Croquet was very popular at the Moody Farm on the Moody Road. The home is now owned by Elwell Gammon, Jr. *Courtesy Limington Historical Society*

Right: Chase reunion, Standish, early 1900s. *Courtesy Standish Historical Society*

Above: Home of William L. Barbour located on Long Hill Road and was later known as the Doughty Farm, circa 1900. *Courtesy Gray Historical Society*

Above: Joshua Small (1836-1912) feeds his hens in front of his home on Pine Hill Road, Limington area. This Joshua was the fourth generation to have the first name Joshua. Harry and Carrie Cotton lived there in more recent years.
Courtesy Limington Historical Society

Right: A team of oxen are pulling a cartload of manure from a barn in Limington. *Courtesy Limington Historical Society*

Above: Jonello Cottage was owned by Loren and Ella Olney and located on the Lower Bay of Kezar Lake. *Courtesy Fryeburg Historical Society*

Above: East Waterboro Free Baptist Church, early 1900s. *Courtesy Sanford Historical Committee*

Right: West Newfield Post Office, early 1900s. *Courtesy Sanford Historical Committee*

Above: Dedication of North Sebago Methodist Church, August 30, 1903. Pictured, left to right are Fred Robinson, Maurice Libby, Paris Ward, Francis Ward, Mrs. J.J. Allan, Asenall Burnell, Nellie McKenney, Mrs. Chas. Jones, Julia Shaw, Helen Jones, Wallace Shaw, Carrie Bacheldor, Flora Shaw, Cora McKenney, Abram Ward, Sarah Ward, Fannie Anderson, Everett Anderson, Lila Bacheldor and Vera Thompson Mauce Bacheldor. In the doorway are Joseph Bacheldor, Rev. McFarlan, O.S. Shaw and Billie McKenney. *Courtesy Sebago Historical Society*

Above: Anna Carey Bradley was a Fryeburg artist known in town for always riding her bicycle wearing baggy bloomers and a large hat carrying her art supplies strapped to her back. She started her art lessons at a very young age and painted all day, every day because her family was well-to-do. She was born in Fryeburg in 1884 and died in 1956. *Courtesy Fryeburg Historical Society*

Right: Construction of the I.O.O.F. Hall Enterprise Lodge No. 36, South Waterboro, circa 1912. *Courtesy Sanford Historical Committee*

Above: This image of Mary Weston Post was taken by her husband, photographer William B. Post (1857-1921). He came to Fryeburg in 1901 and married Mary Webster Weston. They lived at the Fryeburg Tavern where the local fire station now stands. Post was a nationally recognized photographer at a time when photography was growing into an art form.
Courtesy Fryeburg Historical Society

Above: Grange Hall in West Poland, circa 1905. *Courtesy Standish Historical Society*

Right: Town of Gray's Baptish church was decorated for Memorial Sunday by Mrs. Phoebe Leach in the early 1900s. Gray was one of the first towns in Maine to recognize Memorial Day. *Courtesy Gray Historical Society*

Above: Free Baptist Church, built in 1871 at a cost of $5,715. In 1923 it became Calvary Community Church, Harrison. Photo early 1900s. *Courtesy Harrison Historical Society*

Right: Apple picking in the Standish area, circa 1910. *Courtesy Standish Historical Society*

Below: This house on Route 202 in South Waterboro was known as Hotel Enterprise at one time. Photo circa 1905. *Courtesy Sanford Historical Committee*

Above: Sebago Center Church members, June 10, 1909. Pictured are Alex Chessy, unidentified teacher, Emma Lombard, Winnie Thorne, Florence White, Lena Burnell, Alice Miller, Harry Meserve, Harold Decker, Bethesda Bosworth, Mildred Sanborn, Beulah Fitch and Harold Bickford. *Courtesy Sebago Historical Society*

Left: Andrew Andersen came to America from Sweden. He was associated with Loren Olney of Fryeburg. Here he is putting a ring on the finger of his (future) wife, Ada. *Courtesy Fryeburg Historical Society*

Right: Ann Hutchins Andersen, daughter of Andrew and Ada Andersen, who were friends of photographer Loren J. Olney of Fryeburg. *Courtesy Fryeburg Historical Society*

Above: Mark's Corner (Cape Road 35A and Saco Road), circa 1900. On the left is a tavern that is connected to a home and containing the South Standish Post Office. On the right is the Jeremiah Lubly home. Upper right is the carriage shop.
Courtesy Standish Historical Society

Right: Pleasant River House, Jake Morrell's stable before the house burned, and called Morrell's Corner before it became Foster Corner. *Courtesy Windham Historical Society*

Above: Universalist Church at South Windham. *Courtesy Windham Historical Society*

Left: This photograph was taken by Fryeburg resident and photographer William B. Post. Post worked during the years when photography was becoming an art form, and more than just a means of documentation. Post was known for his choice of subjects, for their grace and beauty, and for his unique selection of lighting. *Courtesy Fryeburg Historical Society*

Above and right: Eighteen teams of oxen are needed to carry this heavy load of materials on Route 25 to the Bonny Eagle power house in Standish, circa 1910.
Courtesy Standish Historical Society

Above: Located in the center of Fryeburg's business section, the Steven's Monument was built in memory of early settler John Stevens. He wintered here in 1762-1763. The monument was erected in 1902 by Henry Pierce of San Francisco, the great grandson of John Stevens. It is made of white Hallowell granite, resting upon a base 7-8 feet square and 10 feet thick. On this base rest four large pieces of granite, three bowls for animals and one with a faucet and cup for people. It weighs 28 tons. In 1934, the monument was moved back 20 feet from the original site because of increased traffic. In 1972, the monument was accidentally hit by a truck and badly damaged. It was hauled to Barre, Vermont for repair. A new base was installed with a curbing to prevent further mishap. The photograph was taken by Fryeburg resident Byron E. Emery, circa 1914. *Courtesy Fryeburg Historical Society*

Above: Windham Center Circulating Library, 1920. It is believed to be Walter Peavey in the photo. The library moved in 1973.
Courtesy Windham Historical Society

Above: Helen Douglas Irish, daughter of Ed and Vesta Douglas, owners of Douglas Inn and Douglas Orchards, Douglas Hill, Sebago. *Courtesy Sebago Historical Society*

Left: Ed Douglas spraying fruit trees in the Douglas Orchard, Sebago, 1920s.
Courtesy Sebago Historical Society

Above: Winnie and Patricia, guests at Dyke Mountain Farm. The waitress is Grace Rankin (Brown).
Courtesy Sebago Historical Society

Above: Twin Lake House at Hog Fat Hill in Convene, circa 1924.
Courtesy Sebago Historical Society

Right: Dyke Farm crew, Sebago, 1925. *Courtesy Sebago Historical Society*

Right: Spaulding Memorial Library in East Sebago, 1930. The library was a gift to the town from Mrs. Leon Spaulding. *Courtesy Sebago Historical Society*

Above: Residence built in 1840 by Peter and Almon Young, Sebago. This later became the residence of the principal for Potter Academy. *Courtesy Sebago Historical Society*

Left: Stimson Memorial Hall was built in 1900 and was given to the town of Gray by Captain Theophilus and Mary Stimson's children, as a memorial to their parents. The stage has a proscenium that is probably the only one of its type left in Maine. On the curtain is a huge Venetian scene painted in oil by Edgar S. Caswell, a Gray resident. The building was used for several social activities. The third floor was used as a library and religious societies of the town were to have free use of the building. The building is fronted by Doric pillars and certainly has an aesthetic value. On October 2, 1992 the building was entered in the National Register of Historic Places. Photo taken in 1925. *Courtesy Gray Historical Society*

Left: Sarah Wilson, an eighth-grader at Hancock Junior High School in 1934, won the National Spelling Bee in Washington, D.C. She was the first contestant from Maine as well as New England to win the honor. Photo taken in 1934. *Courtesy Gray Historical Society*

Below: Harrison's Drum and Bugle Corps, organized under the Harrison Volunteer Fire Department in February 1932. It was the only organization of its kind in the world. In the photo, front row: Harry Smith, Harold Maxfield, Harry Maxfield, Ross Catland, Fred Tenney, Bill Burnell, Hobart Denison and Hartley Pitts. Back row: Bill Spiller, Frank Freeman, Eddie Webber, Everett Kangas, unidentified, Phil Spaulding, Gordon Stuart and Bert Davis. *Courtesy Harrison Historical Society*

Above: Matthew Morrill Homestead was a landmark in Gray for many years (located on Route 26). Mr Morrill was a state senator. His grandson discovered a blaze in the barn on July 14, 1929. The fire spread rapidly, destroying the entire farm. Only the household furnishings were saved. Total amount of loss was $20,000. Photo circa 1929. *Courtesy Gray Historical Society*

Below: Threshing oats at the Thomes Farm on Maple Ridge, Harrison, 1930s. *Courtesy Harrison Historical Society*

Left: Percy Bachelder plowed a road for the town on the ice from North Sebago to Muddy River in the winter of 1934-35. *Courtesy Sebago Historical Society*

Above: Paine Reunion at the Old Red Church, Standish, 1930s. In the photo are Carrie H. Malone, Helen Higgins, Gertrude Rand, Eva Allen, M. Higgins, Henrietta Poindexter, Millard Boulter, Harriett Paine, Margaret Higgins, Charlie Paine and Leonard Paine. *Courtesy Standish Historical Society*

Left: Lou Chase entertains with his violin, Standish, February 23, 1936. *Courtesy Standish Historical Society*

Right: Women's State Relief Corps standing in front of Stimson Memorial Hall in Gray, circa 1930s. *Courtesy Gray Historical Society*

Above: Gathering of families for an unknown occasion at farm at Kimbell's Corner in Naples, early 1900s. This farm is presently Reinhard's farm (since the 1950s). *Courtesy Sebago Historical Society*

Right: Harrison 4-H club members, 1938. Pictured, first row: Margaret Butterfield and Marion Day. Second row: Virginia Purington, Aune Heino, Betty Carlson, Jacqueline Reilly and Barbara Peary. Third row: Verna Martin, Pauline Allen, Margaret Wentworth and Lillian Butterfield. Fourth row: leader Margaret Denison, Barbara Reilly, Sally Higgins, Phyllis Briggs, Vivian Ward, Patsy Merrill, Blanche Merrill, Arlene Merrill and Ruth Lundstrom. Back row: Effie May Nesbit, Hilda Chapman, Dorothy Peary, Janet Higgins and assistant leader Edith Bradbury. *Courtesy Harrison Historical Society*

Above: The post office on Main Street in Gray, circa 1939. The post office workers at this time were Lucy Wilson, Elizabeth Douglass and Marion Douglass. *Courtesy Gray Historical Society*

Right: The Dry Mills Post Office was publicized as the "Smallest Post Office in the State of Maine." Postmaster Bernice Prince worked there from 1938 to 1957. When people stopped to pick up mail from one of the 64 wooden, gold leafed numbered mail boxes, many would spend some time chatting with each other before going on with their day's work. *Courtesy Gray Historical Society*

Left: Lou Chase, who spent time around Steep Falls in the Standish area, performed as an organ grinder in the early 1900s. *Courtesy Standish Historical Society*

Seven

Disasters

Reflecting on the tragedies faced by our ancestors, we can only salute their resilience.

For example, the July 1911 fire in the village of South Waterboro – allegedly caused by a man who had had too much to drink, and dropped a cigarette in a stable, though he was tried and found innocent – left 100 people homeless and caused more than $100,000 in property damage, according to a newspaper headline of the day. The town's biggest employer, the Smith Mill sawmill, was destroyed, as were three blacksmiths shops, a number of stores and the Odd Fellows and Grange halls. Firefighters were sent by special train from Portland, but did not cover the 31 miles in time to help, and the blaze spread to timberland south of the village.

No one was killed, but there were many injuries. Also leveled were the new Baptist church, designed by John Calvin Stevens; and the Hotel Enterprise, which was rebuilt and still stands today.

The vintage photographs in this chapter do not only record calamities that have befallen Maine's lakes and mountain region's towns and villages – and their people. These photographs also serve as a valuable reminder to us – to cherish what has not been lost.

Left: During the flood of 1936, the Limington-Steep Falls Bridge over the Saco River was washed away. Each year, the first logs driven down the Saco were those that had been cut to ten, twelve, fourteen and sixteen feet in length and were destined for the mills in Biddeford and Saco. Later, four-foot pulp logs would come downriver for pulp at the Steep Falls mill. *Courtesy Limington Historical Society*

Right: Flooding as seen from White's Bridge, Windman, 1902. The bridge eventually washed away. *Courtesy Windham Historical Society*

Above: South Waterboro rebuilding after a devastating fire destroyed most of the town, July 12, 1911. *Courtesy Sanford Historical Committee*

Above: Ruins from the South Waterboro fire, July 12, 1911.
Courtesy Sanford Historical Committee

Right: Ruins from the South Waterboro fire, July 12, 1911.
Courtesy Sanford Historical Committee

Above: On December 30, 1921, on a cold bitter night, a fire broke out in the hardware store on Main Street and destroyed seven buildings on the east side of Gray village. Bucket brigades were formed. However, they were inadequate.
Courtesy Gray Historical Society

Right: Narrow Gauge train accident at Harrison.   *Courtesy Harrison Historical Society*

Above: Smoldering ruins from a devastating fire, May 14, 1907 in Harrison.   *Courtesy Harrison Historical Society*

Left: Ruins of the chair factory and sawmill after the May 14, 1907 fire.   *Courtesy Harrison Historical Society*

Eight

Celebrations

How fitting that this book – itself a pictorial celebration of the late 19th and early 20th century history of Maine's south and western lakes and mountains region – should conclude with a chapter of celebrations, a tribute to the spirit of the people of these towns and villages.

Looking over these photographs, we may remark that not all are entirely celebratory in mood. For example, the 1930 Armistice Day parade in Gray, and the Sept. 1, 1919 "Welcome Home" ceremony for soldiers from the area who had fought in World War I, are tempered when we consider the town's tradition of military service – and sacrifice. In proportion to its population, in the Civil War Gray supplied more soldiers to the Union cause than did any other town in Maine, with more than one-third of the town's male adult population volunteering. The Gray cemetery houses the graves of 178 Union soldiers.

At the same time, in this chapter we salute an essential, joyful part of the life of the region: the fairs, parades, and festivals; the Old Home Days, the July 4 galas, and the town centennials, so many of which are still celebrated today. These special occasions, like the photographs in this volume, bind us to our past.

Left: Harrison Centennial parade in 1905. *Courtesy Harrison Historical Society*

Right: The decorated wagon of the Elmwood Farm is ready to parade around the track at Gray Fair Grounds, circa 1890. *Courtesy Gray Historical Society*

Above: Harrison Village decorated for the town's Centennial celebration. This area would burn down in 1907.
Courtesy Harrison Historical Society

Right: The Armistice Day Parade in Gray was one of the many parades that American Legion Post #86 sponsored. Photo circa 1930. *Courtesy Gray Historical Society*

Left: Gray Fire Department's fire truck at a parade in the late 1930s. *Courtesy Gray Historical Society*

Opposite page: A July 4, 1919 celebration in Harrison. *Courtesy Harrison Historical Society*

Below: On September 1, 1919, the Town of Gray held a big "Welcome Home" ceremony for World War I servicemen. *Courtesy Gray Historical Society*

Business Profiles

$\mathcal{T}$he businesses profiled in the pages that follow have a long and distinguished record of service to the Maine Lakes & Montains area, and the *Portland Press Herald/Maine Sunday Telegram* wishes to thank them for their contributions to this historical celebration.

A special thanks to Len Libby Candies for its generous support. The third-oldest business in Scarborough, Len Libby will mark its 80th anniversary in 2006.

LEN LIBBY
Handmade Candies
Scarborough, Maine

CLAIR MOTOR GROUP

ESTABLISHED 1964

Clair Motors was founded in 1964 by James E. Clair Sr., "Ernie." Ernie began his success in West Roxbury, Massachusetts, with Clair Buick, a one-showroom dealership that turned into the multi-franchised organization known today as the Clair Motor Group. Ernie's down-to-earth approach, with an emphasis on solid customer service, allowed him to prosper where many others had failed.

Over the past 40 years the Clair Motor Group has grown into one of the largest family-owned dealerships in New England. Through his leadership, Ernie also inspired his sons to continue this great family tradition. His sons, Jim, Joe, Mark, and Michael, are proud to be a part of this landmark organization.

In 1990, James "Ernie" Clair Sr., in part due to his fondness for the State of Maine, opened Clair Volkswagen with his son, Michael. Today, Michael continues the family tradition on Route 1 in Saco, managing the Clair Saco Auto Group.

Clair Ford Lincoln Mercury Mazda, US Rt. 1 Saco, ME 207-282-0300/1-800-442-5247 www.clairford.com
Clair Saco Honda, US Rt. 1 Saco, ME 207-282-0900/1-800-924-9981 www.clairsacohonda.com
Clair Saco Volkswagen, US Rt. 1 Saco, ME 207-283-2900/1-800-742-8425 www.clairvw.com

CLAIR SACO AUTO GROUP

Clair Saco Auto Group is located on Route 1 in Saco, Maine, and has been serving communities in southern Maine since 1990. With three locations, Clair Saco Auto Group offers the New England community a great selection of Fords, Hondas, Lincolns, Mercurys, Mazdas, and Volkswagens.

The Clair Saco Auto Group has been recognized for superior customer service and sales with a wide range of prestigious awards for many years running. Clair Saco Auto Group's philosophy has always been to provide customers with the highest degree of satisfaction and to exceed their expectations in every way. It is a commitment that lies at the heart of everything we do. Your complete satisfaction is our ultimate goal!

We at Clair would like to thank all of you who have helped in making us Maine's largest dealer. Never will we forget that our customers are the No. 1 reason for our success.

Clair Ford Lincoln Mercury Mazda, US Rt. 1 Saco, ME 207-282-0300/1-800-442-5247 www.clairford.com
Clair Saco Honda, US Rt. 1 Saco, ME 207-282-0900/1-800-924-9981 www.clairsacohonda.com
Clair Saco Volkswagen, US Rt. 1 Saco, ME 207-283-2900/1-800-742-8425 www.clairvw.com

COLE FARMS

Cole Farms family-style restaurant was founded in 1952 by the Cole family of Gray, and today is one of the oldest family owned and operated establishments in Maine.

The original restaurant had seating for 24 patrons. After a dozen additions over the years, it now seats more than 350. The upstairs banquet hall and dining room were added in 1986, and now serves the general public, as well as tour and special function groups.

In 1983 Cole Farms' house dressing, long a favorite among regular customers, was bottled for retail sale. It quickly became a hit throughout New England.

In 1999, Spring Meadows Golf Club, built on the Cole dairy farm land in Gray, opened as a nine-hole course. It was expanded to 18 holes in 2000, and today Spring Meadows is noted as one of the must-play courses in New England.

Whether for dining, enjoying a function or after a round of golf, when customers come to Cole Farms, they know they are sharing in a true Maine tradition.

HALL IMPLEMENT COMPANY

For more than 40 years, Hall Implement Company has been the source for agricultural and commercial equipment in southern and western Maine. It all began in February 1961, when George Hall set up shop at the rotary in Windham to sell and service John Deere agricultural machinery. Through the years, Hall Implement Company expanded steadily, and now employs a staff of 15. The company still sells and services a broad range of John Deere equipment, but it also has on hand other products as well, including a large selection of replica farm toys.

The company is now managed by three generations of Halls: founder George Hall, his sons, Donald and Stephen Hall, and a grandson, Derek. Together with their dedicated staff, the Halls continue George's commitment to dedicated service and honest dealings with loyal customers that has made Hall Implement Company what it is today.

KITTERY TRADING POST

ESTABLISHED 1938

In 1938, Philip (Bing) Adams purchased the Kittery Trading Post, a small one-room gas station, for the sum of $4,000.00. As a means of supporting his wife and 14 children, Adams sold fishing tackle, tobacco, candy and gasoline in addition to trading hunting supplies for beef and fur pelts.

Over 65 years later and owned by three generations of the Adams family, Kittery Trading Post is no longer a 360-square-foot one-room gas station. Currently over 75,000 square feet in size, Kittery Trading Post continues to offer an eclectic selection of goods and services, diversifying and expanding its product lines to outgrow and surpass an earlier reputation as primarily a hunting and fishing store.

Today, while treasured favorites such as beaded moccasins, deerskin souvenirs and coonskin hats still remain a Kittery Trading Post tradition, a tremendous, in-depth selection of shooting sports, fishing, camping, hiking, rock climbing, winter & water sports equipment, casual & technical clothing, footwear, and unique gifts await the first time visitor.

KITTERY TRADING POST®

"Clean Rest Rooms," a major selling point for the one room gas station in 1938.

In 1942, the first major addtiion increases the size of the store from 360 square feet to 500 square feet.

LEN LIBBY CANDIES

ESTABLISHED 1926

Len Libby started candy-making as a youth in 1896. He apprenticed under local Portland area candy makers such as Center's Candy, Thomas J. Briggs and Brewer's Confectionary and Catering.

After more than thirty years, he opened his own business in 1926 on Spurwink Road in Scarborough. It became a destination stop for Maine families on their Sunday drive to the country or en route to the three local beaches. Out of state vacationers staying at nearby hotels and cottages frequented the store. Upon returning home at the end of summer, visitors contacted the shop to have candy mailed to themselves or as gifts for others. Business grew quickly, mostly by word of mouth.

In 1949, Len Libby sold the business to three investors who included Dr. Fernand Hemond of West Warwick, Rhode Island. His son, Fern, worked summers at the candy store while attending college, and eventually bought the candy business.

Fern expanded the business in 1952 by building the Route 1 Scarborough store and again in 1956 with the opening of a shop in Portland. His wife, Maureen, joined the business in 1967. Today you'll find Maureen and her family working closely with many loyal employees to uphold Len Libby Candies' highest standards, from the quality of the ingredients to the presentation of the confections.

LEN LIBBY
Handmade Candies
Scarborough, Maine

POLAND SPRING WATER

Poland Spring Water's extensive history begins deep in the woods of Maine. Dating back to 1845, this company brought Maine settlers and respective dignitaries flocking to Poland Spring for its curative spring waters and picturesque setting. In the early 1900's a state-of-the-art bottling facility and springhouse were constructed using Spanish architecture as their theme. No cost was spared to ensure that the highest quality of Poland Spring Water be maintained.

Today these buildings together are known as Preservation Park, housing a dedication to the growth of Poland Spring natural spring water. After a three-year restoration project the facilities, listed on the National Register of Historic Places, were faithfully transformed into an informative museum, cafe and gift shop. Through scientific displays and vintage memorabilia, the museum offers a close-up look at one of Maine's oldest industries. Take a hike in the summer or go cross-country skiing in the winter on over four miles of groomed trails. Admission is free, yet the information gained from a visit is priceless.

Hours of operation: Tues. - Sun., 8 a.m. - 4 p.m.
Closed Mondays and all major holidays.
115 Preservation Way, Poland Spring, ME 04274
For more information: 207.998.7143
Sadie's Place Cafe: 207.998.7146

SCARBOROUGH TERRACE

Scarborough Terrace is dedicated to providing the finest in affordable assisted residential living for older adults. We have been providing professional caring services by trained staff for 10 years.

We are committed to providing our residents with security, comfort, support and activity that will enliven their spirits and encourage them to develop and maintain their independence.

We embrace a holistic approach to meeting the needs of body, spirit and mind.

We view Scarborough Terrace as home and understand that we are entrusted with the responsibility to encourage and support our residents' continued involvement with their family, friends and community. We offer social, religious and academic opportunities while respecting our residents' rights to privacy and self-determination.

We are proud to offer a comfortable home in a secure, supportive environment.

The Scarborough Terrace team embraces each resident and welcomes their friends and loved ones as our extended Scarborough Terrace family.

Springer's Jewelers

ESTABLISHED 1870

When Edmond J. Beaulieu bought the George T. Springer Company in 1925, the Maine-based retail store, which sold jewelry, optical products and a host of other goods, already had operated for more than half a century.

Eighty years later, marking its 135th anniversary, the company now known as Springer's Jewelers continues to thrive. Today, it is owned by a third generation of the Beaulieu family and has its primary location in downtown Portland, with stores in Bath, Maine, and Portsmouth, New Hampshire.

Springer's, which has long since honed its focus to the sale, care and repair of fine jewelry, watches and giftware, has burnished its legacy by adhering to a handful of guiding principles: quality merchandise, fair prices, hands-on service, in-depth knowledge, and honest practices.

From its rich history on Congress Street to its distinctive branches north and south, Springer's has not only survived but flourished, providing quality products and stellar service to area residents and visitors alike.

Portland • Bath • Portsmouth, N.H.

SPRINGER'S

Trusted Jewelers Since 1870

SUGARLOAF/USA

The Sugarloaf/USA Resort attracted its first visitors in the late 1940s when Amos Winter and his friends, together known as the Bigelow Boys, set their sights on Bigelow Mountain to become their playground for the fledgling sport of skiing. When the creation of Flagstaff Lake cut off their access to the mountain, they looked across the valley to Sugarloaf Mountain. By the winter of 1951, Sugarloaf welcomed its first skiers – a rugged group of mostly locals who hiked to the summit of the 4,237-foot mountain peak to ski the lone trail: Winter's Way.

The ensuing 50-plus years brought dozens of new trails, lifts, lodges, and a small city to the base of the mountain. The variety and challenge of the terrain and a well-deserved reputation for copious amounts of snow have elevated Sugarloaf to legendary status with skiers and riders throughout New England and beyond.

The addition of the Sugarloaf Golf Club in 1985 was immediately recognized as a masterpiece of mountain golf courses and established Sugarloaf as one of New England's premiere four-season resort destinations.

Today, Sugarloaf is known as a place for more than just terrific skiing and golf. It is a place where you're not just a face in a crowd, but part of a community of Sugarloafers who hold a special place in their hearts for the memories they've made here.

sugarloaf/usa®